Can We Save Them?

Endangered Species of North America

David Dobson   ILLUSTRATED BY James M. Needham

P9-DUP-472

Charlesbridge

To my wife, Christina
—*D. D.*

For children who find wonder in a blade of grass
—*J. N.*

Text copyright © 1997 by David Dobson
Illustrations copyright © 1997 by Charlesbridge Publishing
All rights reserved, including the right of
reproduction in whole or in part in any form.

Published by Charlesbridge Publishing
85 Main Street, Watertown, MA 02172-4411
(617) 926-0329

Printed in the United States of America
(hc) 10 9 8 7 6 5 4 3 2
(sc) 10 9 8 7 6 5 4 3 2

Library of Congress Cataloging-in-Publication Data
Dobson, David, 1969–
    Can we save them?: endangered species of North America/
by David Dobson; illustrated by James M. Needham.
        p.   cm.
    Summary: Discusses the physical characteristics, habits, natural habitat, and
protection of many endangered species in North America, including Florida
panthers, Puerto Rican parrots, and a variety of wildflowers.
    ISBN 0-88106-823-3 (reinforced for library use)
    ISBN 0-88106-822-5 (softcover)
    1. Endangered species—North America—Juvenile literature. 2. Wildlife
conservation—North America—Juvenile literature. [1. Endangered species.
2. Rare animals. 3. Rare plants. 4. Wildlife conservation.] I. Needham, James,
ill. II. Title. QL83.D65   1997
591.52'9'097—dc20   96-17854

The paintings in this book are done in gouache on Crescent illustration board.
The display type and text type were set in Stone Informal and Souvenir.
Color separations were made by Pure Imaging, Watertown, Massachusetts.
Printed and bound by Worzalla Publishing Company, Stevens Point, Wisconsin
Production supervision by Brian G. Walker
Designed by Diane M. Earley

North America is made up of many different environments. In the far north, in Canada and Alaska, snow and ice are present all year-round. In the far south, in Mexico and Central America, rain forests and steamy jungles cover the land. Between these two extremes, there are deserts, forests, mountains, open plains, lakes, and rivers. Each of these environments is home to animals and plants, but some of these animals and plants are in danger of dying out. In many cases, this is because of a newly arrived animal called *Homo sapiens*.

Homo sapiens is the only kind of living organism—the only species—that lives in all of the different environments of North America. *Homo sapiens* are kind of funny looking. They have big heads, very little fur, small teeth, and they move around by lifting themselves up on their back feet. Maybe you have seen some where you live.

Homo sapiens like to change their environment. They bring in water to grow food, and they cut down trees to make room to live. They build houses, roads, and cities. *Homo sapiens* is also the only species that reads books. I bet you are a *Homo sapiens*.

Most other species cannot compete with *Homo sapiens*. To survive, they move as far away from where we live as they can, or they try to find ways to live with us. Unfortunately, we are not very easy to live with, and there are not many undisturbed wilderness areas left in North America.

We will look at some species that have had the hardest time dealing with *Homo sapiens*. We call these species *endangered* because they are nearly extinct. Let's see what we can do to help these species survive.

Can we save the Florida panthers?

Florida panthers are large *carnivorous* (meat-eating) cats related to the western mountain lion. They eat mainly deer and wild pigs. These panthers like dense vegetation for hiding, hunting, and protecting their young. There is no record of them attacking people, and they rarely attack farm animals. There are only thirty to fifty Florida panthers left in the wild. They live in a very small area of forest and marshes in southern Florida.

Panthers used to live throughout the southern United States, but people have cut down forests and drained marshes to grow fruit and other crops. The panthers are protected by law, but many have been killed by cars while trying to cross highways.

To save the Florida panthers, we need to restore forests and marshes, and we must also protect them from speeding cars. Speed limits have already been lowered on some Florida roads, and a special underpass was built under one part of a highway for panthers to walk through safely.

Can we save the Oahu tree snails?

Oahu, one of the islands of Hawaii, is home to colorful tree snails. Oahu tree snails are part of Hawaiian folklore and songs. They only eat fungus, which they find on the leaves of native Hawaiian trees and bushes. Some of these snails live their whole lives on a single tree.

There used to be forty-one species of Oahu tree snails, but now sixteen of the species are extinct. The rest are in danger of extinction. In the last century, millions of tree snails were collected for their pretty shells, which were used in leis and in jewelry. Now the snails are protected from collectors by law, but this is not enough to save them. They are also threatened by predators such as rats and carnivorous snails, which were brought to Oahu by outsiders.

To save the Oahu tree snails and other endangered species with beautiful shells or fur, we need to make sure we do not buy jewelry or clothing made from them. The snails also need some of their habitat restored so that they can find enough fungus to eat.

Can we save the gray bats?

Gray bats live in many parts of the southeastern United States. They always live in caves near water. In the summer they hunt for insects over rivers and lakes. In the winter they find deep vertical caves and *hibernate* (sleep deeply) through the colder months. They are very sensitive to temperature and will only live in caves that meet with their approval. The population of gray bats in North America has been cut in half since 1970. Almost all of the gray bats now spend their winters in only nine caves. People have forced the bats out of their other homes by blocking off the cave mouths or just exploring them noisily.

To save the gray bats, we need to find more caves for them, and we need to make sure that they are not disturbed during their winter sleep.

You wouldn't want noisy people trudging through your bedroom on a cold winter night, would you?

Can we save the American burying beetles?

American burying beetles are active only during the night. They eat any dead animals they can find, but they prefer birds and small mammals like mice, rats, and shrews. They get their name because they bury the remaining parts of the animal bodies when they are done eating. Though we may find their habits distasteful, these beetles are very special insects. The bodies they bury serve as food for their young and also bring nutrients into the soil. The adult beetles protect their eggs until they hatch, and then they feed and guard their young. Few other insects are so careful with their offspring.

To save the American burying beetles, we should restore natural environments for them to live in, and we can try to move some of them into new areas that they would find suitable. People have also helped the American burying beetles by leaving dead chickens around the areas where they live. The beetles come out at night to eat and bury the chickens.

Can we save the peregrine falcons?

Peregrine falcons are skilled hunters. They feed mostly on smaller birds, which they usually catch and kill in the air. They were quite common in the United States until about 1950, but over the next twenty years they died out almost completely. Most people blame DDT, a chemical used to kill harmful insects. DDT was eaten by the insects, which were eaten by small birds, which were then eaten by the peregrine falcons. The poison made falcon eggshells very thin and easy to break, so peregrines became unable to produce any young falcons. The falcons have been doing much better since DDT has been banned by the United States and Canadian governments.

Some peregrine falcons have found ways to live with people. They have traded tall trees and cliffs, where they usually build their nests, for tall buildings in cities. In cities the falcons can find plenty of pigeons and other birds to eat, but they can be harmed by pollution, roof tar, and poisonous bait set out to kill pigeons.

People are building special nest sites on roofs of big buildings, complete with landing strips and boxes of gravel to keep the falcons' eggs from rolling away. The falcons get nice places to live, and they don't even have to pay rent to the building owners.

Can we save the eastern indigo snakes?

In some cases, if we are lucky, we notice that a species is becoming endangered before its population gets too small. A good example of such a species is the eastern indigo snake. These snakes grow up to nine feet long. Unfortunately, many people capture them to keep as pets because they are beautiful, slow moving, and nonpoisonous. Many stable communities of these snakes live in Georgia near the ocean. We have destroyed their habitat by building houses, farms, and roads, and, surprisingly, by preventing forest fires. The groups of small trees that are home to the snakes need to be burned and refreshed about every five years, or species of bigger trees will take over.

We can help the eastern indigo snakes by protecting their remaining habitat and by allowing controlled forest fires to refresh their communities. We also need to keep people from selling endangered animals as pets.

Can we save the cui-ui?

Endangered fish are harder to save than many other
endangered species. Since fish are confined to lakes and rivers,
they cannot easily move to a new area when they are threatened.

Cui-ui spend most of their time in the Truckee River and in Pyramid
Lake in Nevada, but they need to swim upstream to lay their eggs. In the
past there were so many spawning cui-ui that the fish at the edge of the rivers
were sometimes squeezed out onto land.

Today people use water that would flow into Pyramid Lake for drinking and farming.
This shrinks the rivers and streams that the cui-ui need. Even though cui-ui can live for
over forty years, they need to lay eggs nearly every year to keep their species alive.

We can save the cui-ui and other endangered species that need water by being careful about how much water we use. If we take shorter showers or try not to leave the water running when we do not need it, more water will be left in lakes and rivers.

Can we save the Peary caribou?

People are not always at fault when a species becomes endangered. Some species are too specialized and cannot adapt to natural changes in their environments.

Peary caribou are small reindeer with big feet and antlers. They live in small, widely dispersed groups spread across the islands of northern Canada, far north of the Arctic Circle. They eat as much as they can during the short summer season and spend the rest of the year digging through the snow and ice for buried plants and lichens.

There were almost thirty thousand Peary caribou in the early 1960s, but now their numbers have dropped to less than four thousand.

Severe winters throughout the 1970s killed many Peary caribou and left the rest thin and weak. We cannot save these caribou by changing our behavior because we did not cause their problems. We can try to help them through their difficulties by observing them in the wild and by keeping some of them alive in zoos and animal parks. These are good places to see and learn about endangered species.

Can we save the wildflowers?

Many different kinds of wildflowers are in danger of extinction. Like animals, different species of plants often adapt to their specific environments. When these environments are taken over by people the plants can suffer.

Keeping wildflowers alive is very important. Many endangered wildflowers are very beautiful. Others provide the only food for some specialized insects. Rare plants can also be helpful to people. Many of our medicines come from plants. If we let plant species become extinct, we may be losing sources of valuable undiscovered medicines.

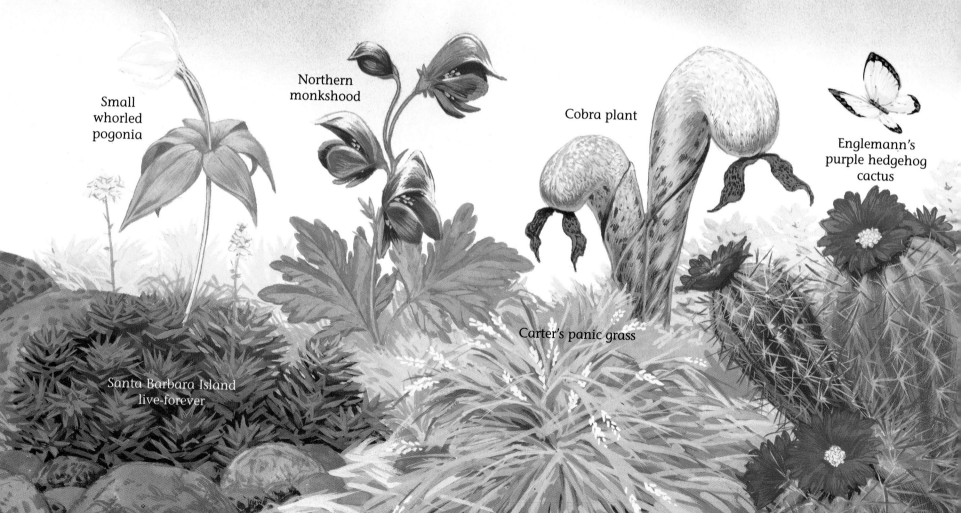

Small whorled pogonia

Northern monkshood

Cobra plant

Englemann's purple hedgehog cactus

Santa Barbara Island live-forever

Carter's panic grass

There are many, many endangered wildflower species. We can help save them by staying on trails when we walk in woods and fields and by being careful not to pick them.

The wildflowers shown here live in very different environments, but they all share one thing—they have silly-sounding names.

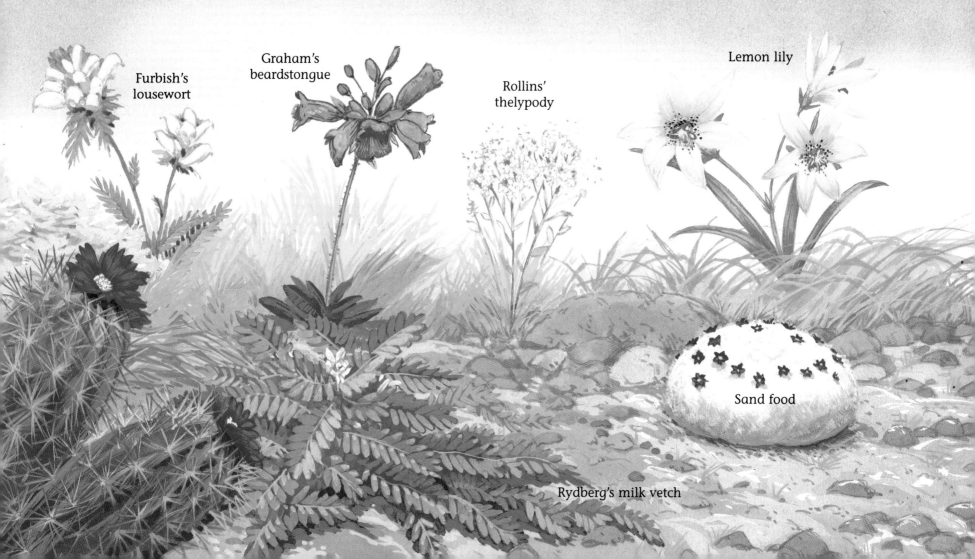

Furbish's lousewort

Graham's beardstongue

Rollins' thelypody

Lemon lily

Sand food

Rydberg's milk vetch

Can we save the eastern timber wolves?

The northern parts of Minnesota, Wisconsin, and Michigan and the Canadian wilderness are the only areas where eastern timber wolves can be found today. They live in small groups of two to twenty called packs. The pack hunts together, which allows the wolves to kill large animals such as moose and white-tailed deer.

Sometimes eastern timber wolves attack livestock such as cattle and sheep. Because of this, some people shoot or trap wolves despite the laws that protect them. The wolves have also been harmed by diseases and lack of wild animals on which to prey.

The best way to save eastern timber wolves in the United States is to provide them with as much open territory with natural prey as possible. Unfortunately, it can be hard to find enough natural habitat for large predators like these wolves. The government and some private groups help to preserve wilderness areas.

If you feel strongly about saving endangered species, you can join an organization dedicated to protecting them. Many people do this by donating money, but it can be more fun to volunteer.

Can we save Kirtland's warblers?

Sometimes a species needs a habitat so specific that both the species and the habitat can be very hard to save. Kirtland's warblers are very picky about where they build nests. Unlike most birds, the warblers build nests on the ground, and they will only build them under jack pine trees. Jack pines only grow after forest fires, when heat from the fires causes their pinecones to open and release seeds. Human beings have been preventing forest fires in Michigan for many years, which has kept the jack pines from growing.

Kirtland's warblers are also threatened by cowbirds. Cowbirds lay their eggs in other birds' nests. Baby cowbirds are bigger than baby warblers, so they get more food from the warbler parents. The baby warblers can go hungry and even starve.

People have helped the warblers by trapping many cowbirds and by burning some forests. Kirtland's warblers are doing much better now because they have fewer cowbirds to worry about and more jack pines to live in.

Can we save the Puerto Rican parrots?

Sometimes an endangered species comes so close to extinction that it cannot be saved without extensive help from humans. Puerto Rican parrots live only on Puerto Rico, a large island in the Caribbean Sea. By 1975 habitat destruction and competition with other birds reduced the number of Puerto Rican parrots to only thirteen.

Scientists worked very hard to help the parrots. They made sure the baby parrots grew up safely and learned to fly by cleaning them off with toothbrushes and by gluing extra feathers to their wings. By 1989 there were eighty-eight Puerto Rican parrots.

These parrots still need much more care to survive on their own, and that care costs money. To help the parrots and other endangered species, you can write letters to your state's senators and representatives telling them how important you think it is to save endangered wildlife.

Can we save them?

Saving endangered species is very difficult, partly because extinction is a natural process. Throughout the history of life on earth, species have been evolving, flourishing, and dying out. Extinctions occurred for billions of years before humans evolved. These natural extinctions can occur for many reasons. Changes in climate, the loss of food sources, new diseases, or competition from other species can all cause a species to become extinct.

Unfortunately for our neighboring species, human beings are unnaturally good at competing. Although our skin is soft, our sense of smell is poor, and we lack fierce claws or sharp teeth, we can use our brains and our tools to help us survive. We can take over habitats and change them to suit our needs. We can cut down forests, plow prairies, build houses and buildings, and use chemicals. All of these things can hurt other species, forcing some into extinction.

There are many things we can do to help save endangered species. We can work to restore natural environments. We can try to conserve our resources, like water and power, and we can recycle much of what we use. We can help to prevent pollution. We can avoid buying products made from endangered species, and we can stop people from keeping them as pets. We can volunteer to work with groups dedicated to saving species and environments.

The most important thing we can do is to learn about endangered species and to share what we learn with other people. We can help endangered species and prevent extinction. When we do, we make the world a more interesting and exciting place for all of us, *Homo sapiens* and all other species, to live together.

Peary caribou
Peary caribou live closest to the North Pole of any reindeer species. Some people have reported seeing these caribou pulling a sleigh driven by an elderly man in red pajamas, but these reports haven't yet been confirmed.

Eastern timber wolves
Some state governments pay ranchers for the damage caused by wolves eating livestock. When saving an endangered species will cost people money or hurt their business, compromises like this one can help both people and animals get what they need.

Kirtland's warblers
The best way to count Kirtland's warblers is by their songs. The male warblers sing very loudly. People count the singing males they hear each year, and the number of singers has been increasing steadily.

Peregrine falcons
In Europe, peregrine falcons have been kept as pets for centuries. Some people would take their falcons out to a meadow or forest and hunt with them for small birds and mammals.

American burying beetles
Sometimes burying beetles fight each other to see which of them will get to lay eggs and bury near a dead animal's body. When the eggs hatch, the *larvae* (baby beetles) are safe underground with lots of food nearby.

Cui-ui
Cui-ui served as a good source of food for Native Americans, especially for the Paiute people, whose name means "fish eaters."

Gray bats
People are often scared of gray bats, but bats are really very good neighbors. They eat many annoying insects like mosquitoes and flies during their summer hunting trips.

Oahu tree snails
At one school picnic in 1853, children collected over four thousand Oahu tree snails!

Florida panthers
In 1982 Florida schoolchildren voted Florida panthers to be the state mammal of Florida.

Eastern indigo snakes
Most Eastern indigo snakes spend the winters in abandoned turtle burrows. It must be a tight fit, because the snakes are six to nine feet long.

Puerto Rican parrots
Hurricane Hugo struck Puerto Rico in late 1989, killing many parrots and destroying some of the forests where they found food. After a few years, though, the parrot population grew rapidly.

Wildflowers
Wildflowers are everywhere! Some treatments for cancer have been developed from wildflowers. Quinine, a cure for malaria, is also a wildflower product.

* Points indicate a primary habitat for each species. Some species do exist in other areas of North America as well.